POTLUCK AT RABBIT HILL

MEMORIES OF LIFE WITH THE
RABBIT HILL BAPTIST CHURCH COMMUNITY

Sigrid Stark

◆ FriesenPress

Suite 300 - 990 Fort St
Victoria, BC, v8v 3K2
Canada

www.friesenpress.com

Copyright © 2020 by Sigrid Stark

Alex Richmond: Illustrations
Daniel DeRegt: Photos
Marilynn Moro: Cover art

All rights reserved.

No part of this publication may be reproduced in any form, or by any means, electronic or mechanical, including photocopying, recording, or any information browsing, storage, or retrieval system, without permission in writing from FriesenPress.

ISBN
978-1-5255-1746-4 (Hardcover)
978-1-5255-1747-1 (Paperback)
978-1-5255-1748-8 (eBook)

1. BIOGRAPHY & AUTOBIOGRAPHY, PERSONAL MEMOIRS

Distributed to the trade by The Ingram Book Company

To Loren, Alita and Mark, Danica,
Daniel and Melissa, and Jonathan

My companions on the journey

TABLE OF CONTENTS

INTRODUCTION
Hem in Your Blessings with Praise Lest They Unravel

FIRST IMPRESSIONS

1	**CHAPTER 1**	Who Burned down the Outhouse?
7	**CHAPTER 2**	Dale and the Ball Diamond
13	**CHAPTER 3**	A Spring Visitor
21	**CHAPTER 4**	Potluck at Rabbit Hill
27	**CHAPTER 5**	The Girls
41	**CHAPTER 6**	Mable
49	**CHAPTER 7**	Country Living
59	**CHAPTER 8**	Secret Sisters
65	**CHAPTER 9**	Hunting Gophers and Tossing Mice
71	**CHAPTER 10**	Uncle Pete and Auntie May
79	**CHAPTER 11**	Worship Special

85	**CHAPTER 12**	
	Smiles Through Tears	
91	**CHAPTER 13**	
	David, Alma, and a Dog Named Caesar	
97	**CHAPTER 14**	
	A Rabbit Hill Welcome	
103	**CHAPTER 15**	
	Uncle Ben and Auntie Lillie	
109	**CHAPTER 16**	
	An Extended Family	
115	**CHAPTER 17**	
	A Rabbit Hill Christmas	
121	**CHAPTER 18**	
	A Gift for Pastor Loren	
125	**CHAPTER 19**	
	Cornflakes in My Bed	
133	**CHAPTER 20**	
	Saying Goodbye	
141	**CHAPTER 21**	
	Potluck Recipes	
	Apple Cinnamon French Toast	
	Auntie Lillie Kuhn's Most Excellent Ginger Snaps	
	Auntie Lillie's Cinnamon Buns	
	Delores' Apple Pie	
	Alma Kuhn's Heavenly Lemon Pie	
	Homemade Oreos	
	Oma's Streusel Kuchen	
	Potluck Baked Beans	
	Pulled Pork	
	Delores' Ice Cream Pail Pickles	

INTRODUCTION

Hem in Your Blessings with Praise Lest They Unravel

RABBIT HILL BAPTIST IS A HISTORIC, RURAL CHURCH that sits just outside the southwest corner of Edmonton's city limits. My husband, Loren, was called to be their senior pastor in January 1992 and served until June 2004, becoming the longest serving pastor in the church's history. In many ways the church served us. They helped raise our children, invited us to their tables, and charmed us with their unfailing laughter. It was an honour to be part of their lives. It was and continues to be evident that they love God and they love us.

This book is a collection of memories of our time with the Rabbit Hill congregation. We've carried the stories around in our hearts and shared them with new friends. When we've had the opportunity to reunite with our Rabbit Hill family, we've remembered our stories together. It is my hope that this book hems in these memories—our blessings—with praise so that they do not unravel.

I am grateful to our Heavenly Father who brought us to Rabbit Hill and continued to give us reasons to stay. There was joy there that we were able to take with us. Loren and I pray that God would show favour on this little church and that He would continue to give them joy and bring others through the church doors who ache for this kind of a community of faith.

I am thankful for my friend, Sharon Tisdale, who encouraged me to write down the stories and has been my Rabbit Hill connection throughout the years. During the writing of this book, she and Karen Kuhn helped me immensely with fact checking and contacting people whose names are mentioned in the stories. Thank you. You understood that no one should be surprised by seeing their name in the book. Thank you to Alita Deepwell for your honest feedback. And a very big thank you to our Rabbit Hill family for allowing me to tell these stories.

FIRST IMPRESSIONS

*There is no such beauty as where you belong
Rise up, follow me, I will lead you home.*

Stephen Paulos, "The Road Home"

Rabbit Hill came into our lives at just the right time. We needed a place where we could catch our breath and heal. We needed a church that gave the pastor time with his young family. The congregation needed a pastor that would see them through their 100th anniversary, which was to be celebrated within months of our arrival. We saw a small congregation with a few people with big hearts and an unswerving commitment to keep the church doors open. They saw a pastor who preached God's Word faithfully, a wife who liked music, and four active school-age children. They saw hope for their little church. Perhaps survival was possible.

Alita, Danica, Daniel, and Jonathan grew up under the watchful and encouraging eyes of the Rabbit Hill congregation. From their first Sunday there they referred to everyone in the church as Auntie and Uncle. The congregation quickly became part of our extended family.

It was a rare Sunday that there wasn't laughter during the service. The laughter told us that these people enjoyed being together in God's house. This was a welcoming place where you could be yourself.

POTLUCK AT RABBIT HILL

CHAPTER 1

Who Burned down the Outhouse?

FOR YEARS MY HUSBAND, LOREN, AND I BELIEVED THERE was a mystery surrounding the fire that destroyed the outhouse behind the church. For some reason, we suspected Auntie Hazel. I don't know where that idea came from, but it seemed plausible enough. She would have been at the church yard cleanup that year; matches were readily available on those occasions, and she would have agreed that the outhouse was unsightly and unnecessary now that the church finally had indoor plumbing. Auntie Hazel was the oldest member of the church then and, like her pioneering parents, understood that if you wanted to get something done, you did it yourself.

Back to the day in question ... I could imagine Hazel making her way nonchalantly over to the outhouse while everyone was busy working elsewhere. As any detective would deduce, she had motive and opportunity.

But it wasn't Auntie Hazel.

It was during an innocent fact-checking conversation with Wes and Delores, Hazel's brother and sister-in-law, while writing this book that the truth was revealed. I asked them if they had any proof of Hazel's involvement or any other clues regarding the outhouse incident. That's when Delores confessed.

"It was me."

"Pardon?"

"It was me and Earl Olsen. Both of us hated that old thing. It needed to go. We had indoor plumbing, and that outhouse was just an eyesore."

Well, that put an end to that mystery and one of the proposed titles for this book. And now I owe Auntie Hazel an apology when I get to heaven.

I remember that outhouse, and those memories are not fond. It was the winter of 1976. As a music student at North American Baptist College I had been asked to play piano and direct the ladies' choir at Rabbit Hill for my first-year practicum. I am sure it snowed every Sunday that winter and the temperature never went above freezing. That's how I remember it.

I learned to watch my fluid intake on Sunday mornings so that I could make it from the dorm to the church and back without having to use that little, unheated outhouse behind the church. The people at Rabbit Hill were wonderful, but I didn't want to linger too long after the service. Occasionally I had a "personal, urgent matter" to attend to. Sometimes the person who had given me a ride would know of my urgent matter and deliberately drive slowly or swerve to hit every possible pothole during the thirty-minute trip on country roads back to campus.

Sometimes Bible school students showed little mercy.

Seminary students were no better.

It was sometime between my 1976 practicum and my return in 1992 that the outhouse went up in flames. I was not in the vicinity; however, had I been there, I would have been a suspect too.

CHAPTER 2

Dale and the Ball Diamond

THIS HAS TO BE SAID AT THE OUTSET. IF SOMETHING OUT of the ordinary happened at Rabbit Hill, it usually involved Dale or a member of his family. One hundred years earlier, Dale's family donated the three acres of land where the church was built, and later the parsonage was added to the property. Today Dale and his wife, Gladys, still own the land that surrounds the church on three sides, and they were our most immediate neighbours.

This is just one of many "out of the ordinary" stories that Dale was involved with during our time at Rabbit Hill. It's one of our favourites.

The 100th Anniversary Planning Committee met and made a list of possible activities for the celebration weekend. Near the top of the list (after the Saturday night banquet and Sunday morning worship service) was a community ball game on the church's ball diamond. All were in agreement.

The small congregation and surrounding farming community loved their Friday night ball games. Auntie Hazel would be the back catcher. Her sister, Auntie Bea, would help the little kids run the bases, and everyone would get a turn at bat. Strikes and foul balls would only be called on those over elementary school age. Everyone understood the rules, even though they had never been written down.

There was one concern about the anniversary ball game. The planning committee wondered if those over elementary school age (who had now grown into strong, young men) might swing too hard and put the stained-glass window on the north wall of the church in jeopardy. Dale offered a solution. He would clear some of the trees on his pasture, which was adjacent to the church property on the east side of the church's three acres. The new ball diamond would face away from the church property, and a pathway would be made in between the spruce and poplar trees that lined the driveway.

The land wasn't being used and, best of all, Dale could clear it with his very big front-end loader. Dale liked big machines. He had a Quonset building full of them, all acquired at various auctions. He and Gladys had their own combines, an assortment of tractors with various attachments, a cherry picker, and other machines I never learned to identify.

And so, one day shortly after the meeting of the anniversary committee, Dale maneuvered the front-end loader to the pasture and happily started knocking down trees. Most of the trees were dead, and it didn't take long to get them piled up in a big heap in the future outfield.

Dale was just about to knock down a smaller tree that was about five feet tall when he noticed the wasps buzzing around it. He put the front-end loader into reverse and made a plan. He waited until dusk when all the wasps were snuggled into their ill-fated home and returned with a pile of rags that he had generously soaked in airplane fuel (how he acquired airplane fuel is yet another story). He stuffed the rags into every crevice of that tree and got a match ready. The wasps inside had no idea what was about to happen. Neither did we.

I was cleaning up the supper dishes when a huge BOOM lifted the kitchen counters and rocked our house. Loren and the kids came running up wide-eyed from the basement to see what had happened. I don't recall that we said anything to each other. We just ran outside where we noticed something burning in our driveway. We got to the smoldering log about the same time Dale came through the trees, wearing his "I've got an explanation for this" look.

The good news was that the wasps were promoted to glory.

The other good news was that there were no cars in the driveway at the time.

We learned that day that a match and enough airplane fuel can launch a standing tree approximately fifty feet. We considered getting the wiener sticks and roasting marshmallows but realized that airplane fuel might leave a bad aftertaste. Besides, we'd just finished supper.

We were standing there, warming ourselves by the unexpected fire and listing all the ways that this rocket could have done more damage when the church's head deacon arrived in time for the monthly board meeting. He joined us at the fire for a few minutes and then went into the church.

A burning log in the middle of the driveway didn't seem to surprise him—maybe at any other church, but not at Rabbit Hill.

CHAPTER 3

A Spring Visitor

AFTER WEEKS OF WINTER DRIVING CONDITIONS, SPRING finally happened. The trees around the parsonage suddenly had leaves, and birds we'd never seen before chirped and chattered from the branches. We were all ready to enjoy our first spring in the country.

The kids and I had just endured another long after-school commute, and they were out of the car as soon as it stopped in front of the house. Every day the four of them would race to the back door where they were greeted by our dog. I could hear Keltie barking as I got a few things out of the trunk and followed the kids. I was at the side of the house when Alita returned, running faster than when she had left.

"Mom, there's a bear in our yard!"

"Really? Are you sure it's not one of Uncle Dale's ..." Before I could finish the sentence with "cows or horses," I turned the corner to see a three-hundred-pound black bear push his way through the wire fence behind our house. Definitely not a cow or horse.

"Go get your father—the rest of you get in the house."

Alita bolted off to the church, opened the door, and shouted her news to her dad. He didn't believe her either but left his office to have a look.

Loren and Alita joined me in the yard to watch the bear wander about in the pasture around fifty feet from the fence. He eventually found a perfect resting place and, within minutes, passed out like a Saturday night drunk slumped up against a tree. I half expected to see an empty bottle next to him.

We looked around the yard and realized the bear had enjoyed quite a good meal from our garbage bins. If it hadn't been for our dog barking from her kennel, he might have stayed around longer.

Dale was the first to arrive, a rifle over his shoulder. A woman who boarded horses at his farm said she'd seen a bear headed our way. She and her boyfriend were the next to arrive. All of us wondered how a bear could find its way to the Rabbit Hill Baptist Church yard.

Before I knew it, our yard was filled with people from far and near to see our bear. How they found out I will never know. This was 1992—long before cell phones announced any bits of unsubstantiated news to the world. Most people in our area didn't even have access to cable TV.

Things were starting to feel like an impromptu block party. I wondered if I should make coffee. Should I put out cookies? Being the wife of a country church pastor was new to me. I didn't know the protocol for welcoming a bear along with the whole neighbourhood to my yard.

Don and Bernice, who lived two farms over, pulled up in their truck. Their sons, Ray and Stewart, who also had farms down the road, were right behind them. Like the others who had shown up, they turned off their engines but left the doors of their vehicles open, just in case they needed to make a quick escape.

By now people were anxious to get a closer look at the bear. After all, he was sleeping; everything would be fine … right? Stewart noticed his mom bending down to go through the wire fence and shook his head.

"Ah, Mom, if the bear wakes up, I'm not coming in to get you. And I don't think you can move that fast."

She saw the sense in that and stayed back. She also remembered that she had a bad hip.

Dale's son David, who lived even further down the road, showed up for a viewing of the bear. Dale fished a camera out of his jacket and handed it to him.

"Davie, here, take this. Get closer for a good shot." He patted the rifle reassuringly and added, "Don't worry, I've got you covered."

David shrugged his shoulders and made his way through the fence. He was just a few feet away from us when Dale whispered to me. "Actually, the gun's not loaded. I'm just using it for the scope."

I realized then that there were at least twenty ways this could end, and none of them were pretty. I went into the house where the kids had been watching from the kitchen window and told them to go downstairs and watch TV. I didn't want them to witness whatever was going to happen. I certainly didn't want them to think that this is how people should react to a bear. I was also concerned about how I would give directions to a rural country church to a 911 operator. We were on a rural route with no street address. Directions were always complicated.

Loren called Fish and Wildlife to report the bear in our yard. It was not a helpful conversation. Their advice was to keep our children and pets inside. Eventually, the bear would find his way out of our area they said. They were not concerned about our neighbour's farm animals. Or the people in our yard.

When I got back outside, I saw that David had made it back to the right side of the fence, and Pete and May had arrived from the city. Pete had a video camera that he wanted to put to good use. Also new on the scene were Minnie, Bea, and Hazel, who were conferring with Pete about getting an action shot. The bear continued to sleep, unaware of the fuss he was causing. Minnie accused me of deliberately feeding the bear a sedative. Why was he sleeping?

Now there were twenty-five ways this could end badly.

Minnie, Pete, and May had been missionaries in Nigeria for years. Clearly, they were missing something of that adventure-filled life. Minnie found an old metal pail and a chunk of brick that she dropped inside. She proceeded to bang and rattle it while the rest of them yelled like the Israelites circling the walls of Jericho.

The bear awoke with a fright and shot up the nearest tree where he was hidden from view. Pete seemed to be pleased with his few seconds of bear action footage and headed back to his car with May, who was still rolling her eyes over what had just happened.

My neighbours started saying their goodbyes. Not in the one-hundred-year history of the church had there been a bear in the yard. It was remarkable they said. It was also time for supper.

The next day we heard that the bear had wandered south to the other side of Highway 19, where he was spotted on one of the Edmonton International Airport's runways. Unfortunately, he was euthanized for being in the wrong place at the wrong time.

Some say he was looking for food. Others say he was looking for a girlfriend. I say he was looking to get away from Rabbit Hill.

CHAPTER 4

Potluck at Rabbit Hill

I OFTEN THOUGHT THE CHURCH'S PHONE NUMBER SHOULD have been 1-800-POT-LUCK and the tag line to go with it should have been, "If you feed them, they will come." If a good, country meal was promised, people would show up. It was certainly true for the 100th anniversary celebrations when the church that only had a handful of members at the time hosted hundreds.

At Rabbit Hill it was common to see someone haul a large roasting pan, salad, AND pie into church on a potluck Sunday. The understanding was that there should be enough for your family and twenty more. Containers of hot food would be wrapped in multiple layers of newspapers or towels to keep warm until the end of the morning service.

Even though we were all supposed to be worshipping, there were two major distractions during the service prior to a potluck. First, the women would be sizing up the crowd and pondering, like potluck hosts the world over, if there would be enough food. At Rabbit Hill there was always more than enough. I am certain that if the women of Rabbit Hill would have been with Jesus when 5,000 people showed up for lunch unexpectedly, there wouldn't have been a need for a miracle. The kid with his little loaves and fishes would not have needed to give up his lunch. The Rabbit Hill ladies would have had it covered.

Second, the rest of the crowd was distracted by the aroma that emanated from the basement. Vents directly below the pulpit sent out whiffs of turkey and whatever else was waiting below. My husband, who has a defective sense of smell, would generally keep to the program. He might have shortened the service minimally by having the congregation sing only three of the four verses of the final hymn. He may not have been able to smell the food, but he could tell when people started getting fidgety, or he could hear their stomachs growling.

Finally, the benediction would be pronounced and, to be efficient, the blessing for the food would be said at the same time. Warm food waiting in the kitchen was hustled to the tables and uncovered. The serving tables at Rabbit Hill were not the usual banquet tables with plastic tops and wobbly legs. These were sturdy wooden tables, built to last and withstand the weight of pots, roasters, and farm-sized serving bowls.

With so much food one had to proceed strategically. After all, as Don Stelter once told me, you can't put ten pounds in a five-pound sack. Good advice. Another man boasted that he didn't waste any room on his plate with anything that was green. This meant bypassing salads and vegetables. He could have those at home. This non-green plan gave him the freedom to layer his plate (rather than section): mashed potatoes on the bottom, meat on top, and then gravy on top of that. And somehow there was still room for a dinner plate full of pie and other desserts.

In my years at Rabbit Hill I never mastered the art of making pie. Why would I need to when I was surrounded by experts who had been perfecting their art for decades? My usual contribution was Mom's recipe for Struesel Kuchen, an easy cake to make with ingredients that were always on hand. When you lived miles from the nearest grocery store, it was important to have a recipe like this in your repertoire.

Even church business meetings were followed by pie. The promise of pie kept discussion to a minimum. I remember our very first Annual General Meeting at the church. Reports were short and informal. The treasurer distributed his written financial statements for review. His verbal summary was the most succinct I've ever heard. "We had money ... we spent it ... now give."

And then the coffee was ready and pie was served.

CHAPTER 5

The Girls

WHEN WE MET THEM, THEY WERE WELL PAST THE "GIRL" stage of life, but that's still how everyone in the church referred to Minnie, Bea, and Hazel Kuhn—three sisters who never married. They were remarkable, independent women with strong personalities and even stronger opinions. Each had succeeded in their own career and had found ways to keep even busier in retirement with things that were important to them: the ministry of Rabbit Hill Baptist Church, the missionary outreach of the North American Baptist Conference, hosting dinners for international students, and keeping the Kuhn clan connected. Surprisingly, ice fishing was also on their list of priorities.

Strong opinions meant that they were not always in agreement, and they were not afraid to verbalize their differing viewpoints, even in front of company. Occasionally they invited us for a meal to their house in South Edmonton. The food was always delicious (except when they served cow's heart) and the conversation robust. Sometimes during a meal an opinion would be offered and discussion ensued. Topics included, but were not limited to, current world events, church issues, extended family concerns, or the price of crops. When you were around Minnie, Bea, and Hazel, you got an education. You also knew instinctively to watch the debate rather than weigh in with your own opinions.

At times things got personal.

It was no secret that Bea despised onions. At potluck dinners people often put a note on the dish that had onions for her benefit. Sometimes they even made a separate onion-free dish just for her. Likewise, it was no secret that Hazel despised the colour purple. She never owned a purple dress and never approved of purple flowers in their garden. These two well-known facts easily became ammunition when one sister provoked the other.

I was minding my own business taking care of the flower beds in front of the parsonage when I noticed Minnie, Bea, and Hazel's car pull into the driveway. Rather than coming all the way down the driveway, they turned right onto the grass and stopped at the "Welcome to Rabbit Hill Baptist Church" sign at the north side of the property. They opened the trunk of the car and started to take out gardening tools and bedding plants. Clearly, they had come to take care of the small flower bed under the sign.

Ordinarily you wouldn't hear conversations at that distance, but not on this occasion. It wasn't long before their conversation became heated. I heard something about purple plants (Had someone dared buy purple plants for the church?), which was followed by "And when you die I'll plant onions on your grave."

As much as they could infuriate each other, they were equally loyal in the face of adversity. When Minnie became ill with what would later be diagnosed as ALS, or Lou Gehrig's disease, Bea refused to put her in the hospital to receive care. She would not hear of strangers taking care of her sister. She finally relented when Minnie was unable to keep her balance. She and Hazel were there with Minnie every day until she passed away.

Hazel and Bea passed away within a decade of Minnie's death. Even though they never had children, they left a legacy that will be remembered for years to come. They cared for others in a determined, practical kind of way. Registrations for children wanting to attend Camp Caroline were quietly paid for. If a child (related or unrelated) was fundraising for a school program, Minnie, Bea, and Hazel purchased the chocolates, cookies, wrapping paper, or whatever was being sold. If a child from the neighbourhood had attended Vacation Bible School at Rabbit Hill, Minnie, Bea, and Hazel made it their business to find out if and when that child performed in a school play or concert. They wanted to be there to cheer them on and let them know that people from Rabbit Hill cared.

I often pictured Minnie, Bea, and Hazel as a train coming downhill through the Rockies. I knew the train was going to deliver something good; it was just safer to stay out of the way.

Auntie Minnie

If you grew up in the North American Baptist Conference, you likely heard Minnie Kuhn speak when she came home from Africa on furlough. For thirty-three years she was a nurse, midwife, and Bible school teacher, first in Cameroon and then in Nigeria. I asked her once how many babies she'd delivered during her career. She told me that she stopped counting at ten thousand. Her presence in both countries was legendary.

From the very beginning the church was proud to have one of their own in faraway Africa and always eager to hear her news. It was in the early years of Minnie's missionary service that her father, Grandpa Kuhn, noticed a letter from Minnie and took it to church, where he passed it to the church moderator to be read during the service. What he didn't realize was that this particular letter was meant for immediate family only. In her letter, Minnie requested in detail what kind and size of underwear she needed her mother to send. Minnie knew nothing of her request going public until she received a package from the moderator containing undergarments. Even though he didn't get the size right, Minnie was thankful for his concern—albeit after she recovered from the embarrassment or, knowing Minnie, the outrage.

Every four or five years Minnie would come home for a year to visit churches and bring news of the work in Cameroon and Nigeria. Back then it was referred to as furlough or deputation. Whatever it was called, it meant a lot of travelling. Somehow Minnie made time for her church and her family, especially her many nieces and nephews. They loved her Pidgin English version of Bible stories, and whatever pictures she brought home. It took Minnie awhile to understand that some of her movies and slides were often a little too medically graphic for most audiences. Not everyone appreciated close-ups of leprosy, burns, untreated eye infections, or facial tumours.

To this day her family remembers Minnie describing how African women gave birth. According to Minnie, the women would hug a tree, push, and, just like that, the baby was born. I doubt that's how it was done in her hospital, but it impressed her enough to mention it many times.

When we attended Rabbit Hill, the ladies still had a traditional Women's Missionary Fellowship, also known as Mission Circle. The main purpose of the group was to correspond with and pray for missionaries. Since Minnie knew many of the missionaries from her days on the field or at various conferences, she helped us pray knowledgeably for the missionaries and their families. She also had great stories. My favourite Mission Circle evening occurred when Minnie told us some "off the record" missionary stories. There were collapsed latrines, a horse that liked to roll over in the river, and creative ways of dealing with church discipline.

After retiring, Minnie continued to champion missions by working on the Northern Alberta Missions Conference, serving as the head of Christian Education at Rabbit Hill, and even going on short-term missions trips to Brazil and Mexico. She lived a powerful life, full of faith and determination.

As a leader in the church, Minnie shared her views broadly. At times she tried to keep her opinions contained, but it was difficult. After one meeting, she told my husband, "I was sitting down on the outside, but I was standing up on the inside."

I have Minnie to thank for giving me the quotation that I use at work when a difficult situation turns out surprisingly well. In similar circumstances she would give a wry smile and say, "God takes care of fools and drunks, and I wasn't drinking."

Minnie received many well-deserved accolades for her pioneering mission work. It was her sisters who kept her humble.

One Sunday Hazel and I happened to be at the entrance of the church when a young woman came in the door. We greeted the visitor, who turned out to be a newly-assigned missionary to Japan and our special speaker that morning. She looked around in awe and said reverently, "I feel like I should take my shoes off. I can't believe I'm in Minnie Kuhn's home church."

Hazel sighed and said, "Please don't mention that to Minnie. Her halo's been a little tight lately."

Auntie Bea

I had a healthy dose of respect for each of the girls, but for Auntie Bea in particular. She worked without ceasing. She was constantly cleaning, moving, serving, and organizing. Even when it wasn't her group's turn to help in the church kitchen, she was in the thick of it. Her other name could have been Martha. Minnie and Hazel would be waiting at the door, and Bea would be making sure everything was in order before they left the church.

She was the smallest of the three but still a powerhouse all on her own. She taught Sunday school, took her turn in junior church, played the organ, kept the church books, and did whatever else that she thought needed to be done.

As church organist, she made it known that she did not appreciate songs in a minor key. Sounded too sad, she said, too "long hair." I was never sure what that meant, but I knew it wasn't something she approved of. Whenever "O Come, O Come Immanuel" was included in the order of service, she played it as quickly as possible, just to get it out of the way. Auntie Bea did not have time for slow, contemplative music.

Before retiring, Bea worked at Transport Canada. I wish I could have seen her in that setting. In retirement she was a decisive, efficient manager. Things got done around Auntie Bea. Like her sisters, she had the ability to see a need and meet it with a practical solution. There was a period when a young woman in the church was being treated for breast cancer. Her chemo treatment had left her bald and feeling conspicuous about coming to church wearing a turban or hat.

As a sign of solidarity, it was decided that all the ladies should wear hats to church. The problem was that most of the women in the church no longer had hats in their closets. Once again, the Kuhn sisters had a solution. They dug around in their attic and found an old box of hats that had once belonged to Grandma and Grandpa Kuhn. They brought the hats to church and left them on the table just inside the front entrance. Each of us chose the hat that went with our outfit that day. I will never forget seeing

Bea at the organ that Sunday proudly wearing a John Deere ball cap, a fitting accessory to her black suit with white trim.

Life with the sisters was a constant recalibration of power. Ultimately Bea was the final decision-maker. She was the one who drove the car, so she decided where they were going. She was the boss. This did not always sit well with Hazel. Even though Hazel was getting older, she still wanted to be useful and help wherever she could with household chores. Bea would tell her that she didn't need to bother; she was getting too old to help and she should just go sit down. Hazel, feeling left out, would phone Delores to report that she needed to take another martyr pill. These imaginary "martyr pills" were just part of life with the girls.

Auntie Hazel

Auntie Hazel made it easy for our kids to relate to another generation. Often after church on a Sunday morning our kids would come home with an Auntie Hazel-ism. When our oldest daughter went to Bible school, Auntie Hazel asked, "So Alita, are there any cute boys at school this year?" When Alita said she didn't think so, Hazel replied matter-of-factly, "Then you should get your money back."

There was a stretch during our son Daniel's teen years that he experimented with various hair colours. The Sunday after he had gone blond he met Hazel at the door. She squinted up at him and announced that she liked it best when his hair was blue. It made him easier to spot in the crowd.

Like her siblings, there was a bit of mischief in Hazel. She and I happened to walk into Edmonton's Jubilee Auditorium together for the closing rally of the Northern Alberta Association's Mission Conference. We were both handed programs at the door, but as she proceeded down the aisle to find her seat, the offering envelope that had been tucked into the program fell out. Trying to be helpful, I picked it up and handed it to her. "You dropped this, Auntie Hazel."

She looked me square in the eye and said, "I did that deliberately."

Hazel's memory always impressed me. Not only did she remember people and events, but she remembered them in balance and in perspective. Once or twice a year the church ladies would gather for a "White Cross" morning when we'd roll up cloth bandages and squares for the hospitals we supported in Nigeria and Cameroon. On those mornings I would try to sit next to Hazel, because I knew stories would eventually come out. The stories weren't necessarily embellished or told in an extraordinary way. They were a bit of history that others had forgotten, or sometimes they were just the other side of the story. Sometimes it was a story about her mother, who also was mighty in strength and convictions. And sometimes it was something from her past. There was that time when a widower with five children from a neighbouring church wanted to marry her. "No thank you," she told him firmly. She saw no need to get married, particularly if he was just looking for a housekeeper.

In the late 1990s, two of Hazel's brothers and one sister-in-law passed away within a short period of time. The Sunday after the last funeral, Hazel arrived at church, and Loren asked how she was doing. She replied honestly that she was not happy. When questioned why, she stated that Ben, Dave, and Ruth had left without her, and she was concerned that the Lord had forgotten about her. After all, she was the oldest of the thirteen Kuhn children who had survived to adulthood. She felt she should have had the privilege of going before the others.

Perhaps it was that Sunday or after another death in the church that she told Loren what she expected at her own funeral. There would NOT be a long eulogy. If things went too long, she threatened to stick her head out of the coffin and tell whoever was speaking to sit down and get on with things. She also didn't want any men as pall bearers. Why? "They didn't take me out while I was alive … they're not going to take me out when I'm dead."

Loren and I happened to be in Edmonton a few years later when we heard that she was in the hospital. We stopped by for a surprise visit and when she saw us at the door of her room, she looked up and asked with a smile, "Are you lost?"

We laughed a little, came into the room, and asked about her health. She made it clear that she was not interested in discussing her health. What she did want to know about was how our children were doing. She asked about each of them by name. At the end of each child's update she asked a few more questions and then nodded in approval for how they were turning out.

A few weeks later, Sharon Tisdale went to visit her Auntie Hazel. Sharon told me that Hazel was glad to have someone to talk to that day. She'd had a dream in which she asked God what kind of job she would do once she got to heaven. God told her that she could take care of the children that no one on earth had wanted.

When she died she wasn't looking forward to a reward of rest ... she was looking forward to her new job of loving children, something she had prepared for on this side of eternity.

CHAPTER 6

Mable

Mable was waiting for me when I opened the heavy church doors on Sunday morning. Her hair was starting to grow back, so the wig she'd worn over the last few months of treatment had been put into retirement. She stood there wearing that bright red suit, carrying a clip board.

"Sigrid, I am glad you're here."

Mable was the only one at Rabbit Hill Baptist who called me by my full given name. Everyone else called me Sig. The kids in Sunday school called me Auntie Sig. Only Mable called me Sigrid. Perhaps she liked the formality, or maybe she just liked being different than the others.

"I'm glad you're here too, Mable." That was the truth. Church didn't seem right without her.

She looked up at me and then glanced down at the clipboard. Mable had a plan and, apparently, I was going to be part of it.

"You've heard that I won't be getting any more treatments."

"Yes, I know."

But really, I didn't want to know. I didn't want to accept that whatever cancer Mable had was going to win. Radiation, chemo, and her strong will had not been enough.

Mable was a tiny woman with fierce determination. There wasn't anything on their dairy farm Mable wouldn't tackle. Plowing, combining, milking … she'd done it all. When Mable was in charge, everything was under control.

"Well, I don't know how much longer I have, so I'm making sure everything is in order for my funeral. You'll sing 'The Holy City.'"

It was not a request. I was being informed.

"It would be an honour, Mable."

I wanted to add that I hoped I wouldn't be called to sing for a long time. I would rather sing with her present, looking up from her usual spot in the front row. Whenever I sang, particularly something out of my classical repertoire, I would get a slight smile and nod that indicated her approval.

However, before I could say anything, she was listing off the others who would be performing at her funeral. The Collegiates, a men's quartet comprised of retired pastors who had all preached at Rabbit Hill sometime during their careers, would sing. A friend from the Edmonton Symphony would play the cello. Loren would preach from the scripture passage she'd already chosen.

I don't recall anything else from that Sunday morning. My mind was occupied with Mable and all she brought to our family. Our kids loved it when it was Auntie Mable's turn to lead junior church. I'm sure there was a Bible story involved at some point, but what they looked forward to the most was decorating cookies. Mable would bring a huge batch of homemade sugar cookies along with several pails of frosting. The kids were each given industrial-sized frosting applicators to decorate their cookies with abandon. Sometimes our four kids were the only ones in junior church, so they were all sugared up by the time church ended. It was a good thing the kids had three acres of land to run around in afterward. They usually didn't require much for lunch either.

Because Mable couldn't bear to have anything go to waste, we were given the leftovers to take home. Kid-decorated cookies went to school for the next week.

Besides junior church cookies, Mable's kitchen produced cakes that would rival any bakery. One Sunday she brought an orange cheesecake with a blueberry topping to a potluck lunch. It was fantastic. I asked her for the recipe so that I could make it for a BBQ we were hosting for our Romanian adoptive families group the following Saturday. Yes, she said, she could do that.

By Saturday morning I hadn't received the recipe and was pulling out the ingredients for Rice Krispee squares when there was a knock on the door. It was Mable. She didn't just bring me the recipe—she brought me a finished cheesecake on a fancy plate along with the blueberry sauce for the top in a container on the side. It looked like something out of a cooking magazine. All I had to do was put it on the table.

I figured she had forgotten to give me the recipe. She figured I was busy enough with four kids and getting the house ready for company that I wouldn't have time to prepare the cheesecake. She was right. It was just like Mable to quietly do something more than requested just because it made sense.

Unfortunately, I've lost the recipe she brought with her that day; however, I will never lose the image of her standing at my door, finished cheesecake in hand. I'm sure that even if I found the recipe and attempted to make it, my cheesecake would never be as sweet as what Mable offered me that Saturday morning.

And now she was planning to leave us. Not that it was her wish to leave early, but it appeared she'd accepted what was ahead with steadfast faith.

Just a month or two after Mable met me at the door of the church, she was in hospice care at St. Joseph's Auxiliary Hospital in Edmonton. Loren and I went to visit her on a Thursday morning. We knew she was getting near the end of her journey and wanted a chance to say goodbye and pray with her and her family. By the time we got there, Mable was unresponsive. We sat with her in the quiet, counting the seconds between breaths. They were coming further and further apart. The hospital chaplain came in and spoke softly to Mable, giving her permission to go, assuring her that everyone was going to be alright.

The quiet was starting to feel uncomfortable so I asked Ron, Mable's husband, if I could sing to her. He gave a big sigh and said yes, that would be fine. I sang "It Is Well with My Soul" and a few other old favourites as quietly as I could. Other joined in as their tears would allow. It is a holy thing to be able to sing someone to the gates of heaven.

We said good bye to Mable, hugged her family, and went home. Within a few hours we received word that she was on the other side of eternity. She was gone; her pain was over.

The funeral the following week went just as she arranged. As per Mable's earlier request, I sang "The Holy City." That song has its challenges even if you're not saying goodbye to a friend and looking at her family while you're singing. As difficult as it was, it was what she wanted, and I was glad to give her one final gift.

CHAPTER 7

Country Living

WE MOVED INTO THE RABBIT HILL BAPTIST CHURCH parsonage on the Family Day weekend in February. Men from the church arrived at our house in South Edmonton with their trucks and trailers and moved all our earthly goods to our new home next to the church. That was Saturday. On Sunday we attended church and on Monday the churches hosted an outdoor skating party at the Shalom Water Park down the road.

Since it was snowing on Monday, I assumed that the skating party would be called off. I was wrong. People at Rabbit Hill would not let a little snow get in the way of a good time. But it wasn't just a little bit of snow. It was a lot of snow that came down in big, fat flakes. A few of the men brought snow shovels and kept clearing the ice while everyone skated around them.

Even though we were out in the open, it was important that a skating party have food and drink. Hot dogs and hot chocolate appeared. The snow was relentless. At least an inch of snow accumulated at the end of my hot dog by the time I made it to that end. People were determined to have a good time. They'd lived through far worse than a little snow on their food.

The following week we tried to get into a routine. Loren drove Alita, Danica, and Jonathan to school in the morning, and I drove Daniel to kindergarten in the afternoon. I would wait in town until it was time to load them up for the homeward journey. This worked most of the time, but during that first week the snow we experienced on Family Day persisted. To make matters worse, the fog rolled in just as Daniel and I were heading into the city. Visibility was less than limited and then it started snowing even more. When I got to the school, I pulled the kids out early and headed home, praying all the way.

We made the turn off of Ellerslie Road—wonderful! We passed Ron and Mable's farm—almost there! Just before the final turn, our car plowed through deep snow that had drifted across the road, and then it died right in the intersection. I could see the lights of the county school bus coming at us in one direction and something else big coming from the other. We needed to do something.

Alita, being the oldest at eight years old, reluctantly left the car and bravely set out through the snowdrifts to get her dad, who was in the church office. A neighbour whom we hadn't met yet came to our rescue even before Loren could get to us. The hood was opened to reveal a snow-packed engine. Somehow we got to the house, and our car was towed to another neighbour who had a heated shed. Two days later, my car was returned in perfect working order.

Surprisingly, in the seven years we lived in the parsonage, I only recall two or three days when the kids missed school because of snow. Loren said we could declare a snow day if he couldn't get the car out of the garage and onto the main driveway. Every snowy morning the kids watched from the dining room window, hoping that the little Honda Civic would get stuck. To their dismay, more often than not, Loren's determination and skill in winter driving conditions meant that they had to go to school.

Since we lived on the church property and the church was considered a public building, the county would send in a grater to clear the driveway up to the end of the church yard. The snow would be shoved in a big pile behind the church to the west of the garage. This giant snow pile became our private sledding hill. After a long trip home from school, the hill was a great way to expend some energy and have some outside fun.

One year we had an enormous amount of snow and we were just barely able to keep the driveway clear. Loren became concerned with the snow that was accumulating on the roof of the parsonage. He and the kids climbed up the ladder and shovelled off as much as they could. While I was inside worrying about their safety, they were on the roof carving up snow and ice to create a little igloo. Just for fun.

Once the snow was gone, the three acres were one big playground. The kids would spend hours outside creating their own games and adventures. For the most part, we could see what was going on from the house, but sometimes not. Nearly two decades after moving from the parsonage, Daniel told us that he and his friend, Joel, would climb one of the spruce trees that ran parallel to the driveway. Then they would try to get from one tree to the next without descending—swinging along like monkeys. Their goal was to get to the tree that lined up across from the cement pad in front of the church. This could take a long time and, as boys would have it, they didn't bother coming down if they needed to pee. It was a good thing we didn't know. My mother used to say that Daniel needed extra guardian angels.

Danica was drawn to those trees as well. There was a magpie nest at the very top of one of the tallest trees, and she was determined to explore it. She'd heard that magpies collected shiny objects and hid them in their nests. Danica wanted to find out if this was true. Unfortunately, the branches didn't cooperate, and Danica fell. Thankfully, she wasn't hurt. She landed with a few scratches, covered in twigs and angry that the tree had let her down. When we moved to the country we decided we needed a dog that would alert us when someone was on the property. Keltie came to us with lots of promise. She loved children and had lots of energy. Too much energy as it turned out. As a border collie she needed to herd animals, so she would routinely make her way over to Dale and Gladys' farm next to the church to organize their horses and cows. Rather than cause trouble with our neighbours, we gave her away to a sheep farm where they could make good use of her instincts.

Before Keltie left she gave us a pup that we named Wolfgang. This was the dog we needed. From Monday to Saturday he barked whenever there was someone he didn't know on the property; however, on Sundays, when people came to church, he would not bark. It was his day of rest as well.

Wolfgang could sense when you'd had a bad day. I would come home from a long, stressful day and sit down on the back step to have a few minutes with Wolfgang before heading inside to whatever awaited me there. He would nudge his head up against my elbow and give me the quiet assurance that it was all going to work out.

Our animal collection grew. We had numerous cats, a rabbit, and a hedgehog. All but the hedgehog lived outside. Loren built a kennel for Wolfgang behind the garage, and on extremely cold days, the cats moved in with the dog. Esther the rabbit, who lived in her own shelter by the back door, appeared to have a personality disorder. Even though we fed and cared for her, she didn't like us; in fact, we learned from her that rabbits have the ability to growl. For some reason she tolerated Danica.

Abby the hedgehog was also a problem pet that hissed. She lived in a cage in the downstairs hallway, and Danica was her primary caregiver. I still prefer cats and dogs over hedgehogs.

One summer Alita, Danica, and I were home by ourselves for a few days while Loren and the boys drove Loren's mom back to her home in Abbotsford, B.C. The three of us made some "girls only" plans, which included a fancy lunch at the Hotel MacDonald in downtown Edmonton. Alita and I were getting ready when we heard Danica screaming downstairs. Abby had died.

I did not like it when animals died on my watch.

When Danica calmed down, we decided to bury Abby somewhere nice on the property. We got shovels out of the garage and looked around. Danica suggested the bottom of a big tree on the west side. This seemed like a nice and reasonable idea until we attempted to dig. Big trees have big roots. Our collective mourning on the passing of Abby turned to frustration, as the three of us couldn't find a place under any of the chosen trees where we could dig. We finally buried Abby in the outfield of the ball diamond. Although the funeral caused a slight delay in our plans, we were still able to enjoy lunch at the Hotel MacDonald as planned.

The children learned that living on an acreage had its benefits. Where else would your parents get you out of bed to see the northern lights? Sometimes a neighbour would alert us, or Loren would notice them on his way across the yard after a meeting. We would wrap up in our blankets and go out in the night to watch the magic colours dance across the sky.

Although the kids could have attended the county school in Leduc, we chose to keep the three older children in the German bilingual program they had been part of before our move to Rabbit Hill. Jonathan attended the county school for two years but then it became necessary for him to attend a city school that could better accommodate his learning needs. This meant that we needed to provide transportation. At any given time, the kids were in two or three different schools, requiring a one-way commute of at least forty minutes.

Most days everything worked well and everyone cooperated. We listened and sang along to the mixed cassette tapes that Alita created. There were conversations and opinions expressed about what was learned or experienced that day. We played car games like the license plate alphabet game or our own version of "zip," a game we learned from Uncle Wesley.

Some days, though, after being in a car after a long day in the classroom, the Stark kids could get on each other's nerves. Loren and I would do our best to keep the peace. There were warnings by us, whining by them. We would announce "quiet contest!" The first person to speak lost the game. When they were older and bickering, we would pull over and ask if the kids knew the way home from that point. In other words, they could walk or be nice. Usually this was enough to get them to quiet down, but sometimes they couldn't wait to get out of the car, even if it was with the sibling they had been fighting with. Sometimes they didn't need a reason to be let out; they just wanted to walk. We were always fairly close to home and would keep an eye out for them once we got to our driveway.

When they exited the car, they explored and observed. On one occasion when Alita and Danica were on one of those walks home, they were certain they saw a dead porcupine on the side of the road. Closer inspection revealed that it was just a clump of mud and straw, but still, it fooled them. Why not try fooling others? They dragged the clump onto the middle of the road and watched from the ditch as motorists tried to dodge the bogus porcupine carcass.

The kids were up for almost any adventure on the property; however, there was one place they never wanted to be on their own—the church. The old building would creak and groan and sound rather spooky if you were there by yourself. One evening when Daniel and Danica were playing games on the computer in Loren's office at the church, they heard a crashing noise from the basement. They carefully went downstairs to inspect what had happened. For some reason still unknown to us, the metal hangers on the coat rack all decided to fall on the floor. They raced each other home.

We learned that there was no such thing as "quiet country living." There was always something going on. There were coyotes that howled at night. When it wasn't coyotes, it was a fox taunting our dog from the pasture. There were feuds between the magpie and squirrels in the trees behind the house. During harvest we heard combines operating around us all night, doing their best to get the crops in before the first frost. And occasionally, one of Uncle Dale's cows would stroll over to have a look in Alita's bedroom window.

Surrounded by farms and having friends who were farmers, we became keenly aware of how much work it took to get food from the field to our table. When a storm would pass through, we would pray that crops wouldn't be damaged by hail. And when farmers thanked God for a good harvest at Thanksgiving, we all said "Amen."

CHAPTER 8

Secret Sisters

MY FIRST MEETING WITH THE LADIES OF THE RABBIT Hill Mission Circle was in January of 1991. On the program that night, as it always was at the January meeting, was choosing our secret sisters for the coming year. We each put our names, as well as our birthdays and anniversaries, on a piece of paper. The papers were put in a bowl and then we picked out the name of the woman for whom we would pray for the next year. Another woman in the group would get your name and pray for you. Of course, this was all to be done in secret.

It felt good to know that someone would be praying for me. I knew that when people from Rabbit Hill prayed, God listened. They had a way of getting His attention.

Along with praying, there was an understanding that you would give your secret sister a small gift on special occasions, such as Valentine's Day, Easter, Thanksgiving, and her birthday and wedding anniversary. Gifts would be left in the church on the table that was nearest the entrance before you went upstairs toward the sanctuary. Since the gift giving was also to be done in secret, there was the challenge of getting the gift you were bringing from your car to the gift table without your secret sister finding out your identity.

The big secret sister reveal would be part of the meeting the following December. This meant that there would be a lot of guessing for a full year. My kids would keep an eye out for anyone who would be bringing a gift to the table the Sunday prior to my birthday in November. Somehow it arrived at the table without anyone seeing how it got there. Once I brought the gift home, the kids would analyze everything about the packaging, the card, and the gift itself. Some secret sisters resorted to disguising the handwriting so that their identity would stay secret until Christmas. One year Delores sent her new secret sister a calendar in January and signed the card, "Your Secret Sister, Delores." There wasn't much guessing needed after that.

Secret sisters were dedicated to keeping their commitment to each other. Even when they were travelling or couldn't be in church, they made arrangements for their gift to be delivered. Sometimes they even asked the pastor to make sure a gift got to its intended sister.

This was never truer than that evening in October when the phone rang and we were told that Debbie had passed away. The cancer she had been fighting had won. Even though we had been expecting the news, the awful, raw truth of it was hard to bear. We went over to their farm and sat with her family, talking about her valiant fight, trying to imagine life without her. All the while we tried to ignore the fact that it was the Friday of Thanksgiving weekend.

When it was time to go home, Debbie's mom approached me with a basket full of little treats, a small stuffed bunny (for Rabbit Hill), some chocolates, and a tiny, wooden, white church—a replica of Rabbit Hill.

"Debbie asked me to give this to you for Thanksgiving. She was your secret sister."

CHAPTER 9

Hunting Gophers and Tossing Mice

ABOUT A YEAR AFTER WE MOVED TO VANCOUVER, Daniel invited some of his new city friends to join us for lunch after church. After the meal, they contemplated possible activities for that sunny, spring afternoon.

"I feel like shooting gophers," Daniel said wistfully.

The guys around the table couldn't believe what they'd heard and asked what he intended to use to shoot said gophers.

"A gun!" he answered emphatically. Honestly, how else would you shoot gophers?

After further questioning, Daniel explained that most of the people in our last church had a gun. Most had guns (plural), as in a collection. Even the deacons? Yes, even the deacons, if they were farmers.

In the city the only people who had guns were the police and gangs. It was a new concept to our guests that farmers might need a gun. Daniel and Loren explained how guns were used on the farm, including for controlling the gopher population on the fields. This also explained why Daniel and Loren would occasionally go out and shoot gophers on a sunny Sunday afternoon. It seemed like a perfectly reasonable activity at the time.

The eradication of small rodents led Daniel to another story. Even though this happened right under our noses, it was a new story to us and rather shocking to everyone around the table. We knew the beginning of the story well enough. Every spring, members of the Rabbit Hill congregation would gather on a Saturday morning for the annual church yard clean-up. Everyone would work throughout the day clearing dead branches, burning off bits of debris, and generally making the three acres presentable. After a day of work, everyone would gather, sometimes slightly singed, around the fire pit for the first wiener roast of the season.

Usually Wes Kuhn had a list of things that needed to be done, but on this particular day, Daniel and his buddy Joel had their own idea of what needed to be done. As far as they were concerned, the church yard included the ditch near the road … and the mice that lived there. Those mice needed to be dealt with.

They devised a plan that only ten-year-old boys would think of and no parent would ever approve. They borrowed a couple of sturdy metal wiener sticks that were waiting in the garage for the evening's wiener roast and made their way to the ditch. No one noticed them, and if they did, they didn't question them.

It didn't take much work to get the mice to come out from their nests. Just a good stomp with their feet, and the mice came scurrying out. This is when the wiener sticks became spears. If any animal rights people are reading this, please understand that we knew nothing of this at the time.

Once the mice had been skewered, the boys needed to find a place to dispose of them. They stayed hidden in the ditch and watched for approaching vehicles. When a car got close enough, the boys tossed a mouse at it like it was a grenade.

Eventually they ran out of mice and made their way back to the garage, where they put the wiener sticks back into the metal pail. They did not wash the wiener sticks nor did they inform anyone else that they should probably be washed. They simply chose to go vegetarian that evening, enjoying the bun without the wiener.

Daniel barely finished telling us the story before I was on the phone calling Pastor Lee, who was living in the Rabbit Hill parsonage with his family. Fighting back the urge to gag, I gave him the briefest version of the story and made him promise to go and wash those wiener sticks. Pastor Lee knew Daniel and wasn't surprised. He promised me he'd take care of the wiener sticks. The story has since been shared with the congregation, and, despite knowledge of that fateful day, Rabbit Hill still holds wiener roasts.

If any child psychologists or therapists are reading this, you will be relieved to know that Daniel and Joel have grown into fine, compassionate men. When they were in their early twenties, they shared a house where they also cared for a turtle named Walter and a kitten named Charlie. As far as we know, there have been no further incidents involving mice.

CHAPTER 10

Uncle Pete and Auntie May

PETE AND MAY SCHROEDER FIRST CAME TO RABBIT HILL in 1954 while Pete was studying at the Christian Training Institute, or CTI as it was known to the young people in the Edmonton area. When he graduated in 1960 as CTI's first theological student, he was ordained by a council called by the Rabbit Hill congregation. From there Pete and May and their family went on to plant churches in Western Canada and serve as missionaries in Cameroon and Nigeria. They eventually returned to Edmonton when Pete retired from full-time ministry.

In 1990, Rabbit Hill needed an interim pastor, and Pete and May agreed to come for as long as it took to find a new pastor. Church attendance was dwindling and there was talk of the congregation folding. It was hard to imagine that the church that had given so many young pastors their first opportunities to preach, generously supported missions, and assisted young churches in the area financially, was seriously considering closing its doors.

Pete convinced the church to keep those historic doors open—at least until their 100th anniversary in 1992. Pete and May decided to keep attending Rabbit Hill after Loren took on the role of senior pastor. The congregation showed their appreciation by naming Pete their Pastor Emeritus, which kept Pete involved in a volunteer pastoral role. The encouragement and wisdom the Schroeders brought to the church could not be overestimated.

Just after we arrived at Rabbit Hill, there was a church membership meeting at which the upcoming Northern Alberta Missions Conference was announced. This conference was a big deal for the Alberta Baptist Association and particularly for Rabbit Hill, who'd led the way in supporting and sending missionaries for decades. One of the weekend's events was a potluck breakfast that was hosted at one of the association's larger churches in the city. All churches were given instructions as to what they should bring to the breakfast: Attendees from Edmonton's surrounding churches were to bring muffins or other baking. Everyone within Edmonton's city limits was to bring a hot dish. When this was announced, Pete put his arm around his wife of more than fifty years and proudly announced, "This is my hot dish."

Pete's sense of humour and adventure was a good fit for the Rabbit Hill crowd. There was always something that needed to be done on the church property, and Pete was ready to lend a hand. At one church picnic, someone noticed that the top of a large tree on the west side of the church yard had partially snapped and was dangling dangerously to one side. A good wind would likely bring it down, and do damage on its way—particularly if it went in the direction of Dale Stelter's machine shed on the other side of the trees.

While the ladies chatted around the fire pit, Pete went to his car and pulled out a machete. I do not know why Pete carried a machete around in his car … perhaps in anticipation of such a chore, or maybe it was just a habit from his days in Africa. He marched past May with his eye on the tree in question. May, without even looking up, said, "Don't even think about it, Pete." Pete stopped, sighed, and let others take care of the tree. Occasionally Pete's boyish sense of adventure needed May's sense of reason. It made their marriage work.

At Pete and May's fiftieth anniversary, we were enlightened to learn an important secret to their long and happy marriage. Pete's nephew, who emceed the event, said that he had asked his uncle for his secret to a successful marriage. Pete's answer surprised him and the rest of us. Apparently early in their marriage, Pete and May agreed that they would never go to bed angry, and that if they were going to have an argument, they would do so in the nude. Once in that state, both of them had difficulty remembering what the argument was about.

As Pastor Emeritus, Pete would often preach when Loren was away. Although May held Pete's affection, it didn't take our children long to pick up on Uncle Pete's other love—airplanes. Inevitably an airplane-related story would work its way into his sermon. The kids would wait for it. They may have even timed when it would appear. His story collection included experiences in the Second World War, building an airplane, and the use of GPS. Somehow Pete could find an airplane-inspired story to illustrate any passage of scripture, Old or New Testament. It was his gift.

When they were in their seventies, Pete and his brother, Henry, built a small plane of which they were extremely proud. It wasn't made for speed (you could drive to Calgary faster than this plane could take you), but it was steady and trustworthy. Or so we chose to believe.

Other churches offered badges and gold stars for children who memorized their Bible verses, but Rabbit Hill offered a free ride in Uncle Pete's plane. The children learned their memory verses, and the parents (at least I did) practiced praying when the little Cessna 150 took off with one of our children aboard. There was only enough room for one passenger and Uncle Pete the Pilot, so there were numerous takeoffs and landings that Sunday afternoon. As was Rabbit Hill's custom, the ladies brought snacks along for parents, children, and other spectators. How else were we going to pass the time?

One Sunday morning, Loren was away and Pete was scheduled to preach. The weather felt unsettled. Anyone who'd lived in Alberta long enough knew there was going to be a storm later in the day. The service went ahead as planned. After the hymns were sung and the offering was taken, Pete launched into his sermon. As many preachers do when needing to emphasize a point, he used his index finger and aimed at the congregation. He uttered that beloved phrase used by many preachers: "and the Lord said." On cue, timed perfectly with his pointed finger, God complied with a simultaneously bang of thunder and a flash of lightning. A shocked silence followed, with Pete's finger still pointing at the congregation like a smoking gun. After a moment he pointed his finger back to himself and mused, "Well, that's never done that before."

He's a preacher with power, our Uncle Pete.

CHAPTER 11

Worship Special

Rabbit Hill Baptist had as many traditions as one would expect of a hundred-year-old congregation. One of those traditions was the involvement of all regular attendees on the worship special schedule. A worship special was expected for every Sunday morning service.

There were no guidelines for worship special. It was just understood that worship special should feel comfortable and appropriate in a country church setting. Talent was not necessary. Sometimes it was a favourite song played from a CD, or a poem would be read. Caroline always found a story in one of her *Chicken Soup for the Soul* books. Beginner piano students played their first solos, which would end with the congregation's enthusiastic applause.

Often one person from the family, the whole family, or a friend of the family would sing. It was quite normal for the soloist to discreetly pass Colleen Stelter the music at the piano as they made their way to the platform. She would quickly glance at the song and accompany them as if they'd actually rehearsed. Colleen's ability to sight read was astonishing.

Auntie Lillie preferred not to sing solos, but she liked it when I did. When it was Lillie and Ben's turn for worship special, Lillie would ask me to sing, which was my joy too. The song choice was usually mine, and I tried to find a hymn that fit with the sermon Loren was preparing. Sometimes Lillie would request "His Eye Is on the Sparrow," which was a mutual favourite. I sang the verses and invited the congregation to join me when we got to the chorus:

> *I sing because I'm happy*
> *I sing because I'm free*
> *For His eye is on the sparrow*
> *And I know He watches me*

Singing was no hardship for me, but Lillie felt compelled to say thank you in a way that our whole family appreciated. At the end of the service, Loren would find a small brown paper bag filled with her ginger snap cookies in his office. When Loren told her they were his favourites, she started leaving two bags— one for him and one for the other five people in our family. We survived.

Early one Sunday morning as Loren was preparing for the service, he overheard Dale rehearsing his worship special in the sanctuary. After listening for a few minutes, he asked Dale to be prepared to sing it at the end of his sermon rather than after the offering, which was the worship special's usual spot on the program. The song, an old gospel tune, fit perfectly with the sermon. Loren instructed Dale to come forward when he finished preaching. The song would help people remember and reflect on the main points of the sermon.

All went according to plan. There was congregational singing, an offering taken, announcements made, and the sermon preached. Dale was at the pulpit on cue. He put his music down in front of him and reached into his suit pocket for his reading glasses. As he did so, he paused and looked thoughtfully over the congregation. Before Colleen could play the introduction, he added his own thoughts.

"I just want to say something. This morning Gladys said to me, 'Dale, you look better without your glasses.' And I said, 'Gladys, you look better without my glasses too.' "

And that's how the service ended. To this day, no one can remember the song or the sermon to which it was related. All we remember is Dale's benediction, Gladys shaking her head in disbelief, and the laughter that rang out in what could have been a sacred moment.

I think God was shaking his head too.

CHAPTER 12

Smiles Through Tears

Loren came into the house during breakfast to give us the bad news. Oma Haut had passed away during the night. The kids were quiet and then the tears started. With the tears came the memories.

When someone in a small church passes away, it feels like a death in the family. Everyone who attended had their own spot—and now Oma Haut's spot would be empty. Oma and Opa Haut sat on the left, about three or four rows from the front. We couldn't imagine Opa Haut sitting there by himself.

Oma Haut loved us with generous abandon. She would ask if she could take the kids for a weekend, and there would be no end of adventures on their acreage. In the evenings she taught them how to play Dutch Blitz and created crafts from the bits of things they had collected during the day. Delicious and comforting German meals flowed out of her kitchen. At Christmas, a big basket full of thoughtful and fun gifts was delivered to our front door. With our own parents in another province, Oma and Opa Haut were an added set of German grandparents.

The introduction to Dutch Blitz moved through our family and beyond. Our kids taught their cousins, and family get-togethers wouldn't be complete without a few raucous rounds of the game. I'm imagining Oma Haut's smile were she to know that years later Danica would bring Dutch Blitz to the research centre in Borneo where she worked. Opa Haut was usually at the periphery of visits to the acreage. He was a gracious and polite host but left Oma Haut to her role of Director of All Activities. Occasionally she would convince him to attach his specialty-built wagon to his horses and take everyone for a ride. When he was out of earshot, Oma referred to the wagon as his "Kartoffelwagen" (potato wagon). Nonetheless, he loved his horses and loved introducing them to others.

Oma Haut had been struggling for a few months. What should have been routine surgery had revealed pancreatic cancer. There would be no cure. And now she was gone.

Jonathan, who was about seven years old at the time, was the first to speak.

"Let me get this straight." He looked up at us to make sure we were listening. "Oma Haut is in heaven now?"

"Yes, she's in heaven."

"So we're just sitting around here feeling sorry for ourselves?"

It was true. But we all needed to feel sorry for ourselves for a while.

The funeral was held at the Ellerslie Road Baptist Church. Our little sanctuary would not have held all the people who had benefitted from her love. It was a beautiful service. We sang her favourite songs. We talked about her faith and allowed ourselves to be sad and hopeful in the same space.

After the funeral, everyone made their way to the Rabbit Hill Baptist Cemetery, about fourteen kilometres away. We gathered around the grave and waited for the rest of the procession to arrive. Even though we believed we would see Oma Haut in heaven, there was a horrible finality to death on this side of eternity. It was painful to look at that open grave while waiting for everyone else to gather around. That's when Armin, one of Oma Haut's grown sons, ventured to look up instead.

"Hey, look." Everyone's eyes went up to the tree that shadowed the grave. There was a smile in his voice. "Mom will be able to do crafts forever with all those pine cones!"

And then there were smiles through tears.

Eighteen months later, Opa Haut would die of an unrelated cancer. Their family and their community were devastated. Opa Haut was a visionary and invested much into the creation of the Shepherds Care Foundation. As a former minister, he encouraged Loren at every opportunity. He often said how glad he was to be part of a smaller congregation where he could greet the pastor personally each Sunday.

Both were models of welcome, leadership, and encouragement. We were honoured to be part of their journey.

CHAPTER 13

David, Alma, and a Dog Named Caesar

SOMETHING THEY DON'T TEACH YOUNG PASTORS IN seminary is how to approach a farm dog. They are there for a reason. They don't care about your theology degree or your good intentions. Unless someone more important tells them otherwise, they want you gone. Loren learned early in his time at Rabbit Hill that farm dogs ruled. If he was going to pay a visit to a farm, he would drive on to the property, honk the horn, and stay in the car until someone came out and called off the dog.

The dog we will always remember was Caesar. He was in command of Dave and Alma Kuhn's place and roughly the same size as our Honda Civic. He may have appeared friendly, but when a dog is big enough to look into the window of the car without having to get up on his back legs, you have to show respect.

Alma or Dave would eventually come out, call Caesar, and welcome us into their place. Dave and Alma were one of the couples in the church who made sure we weren't alone on special occasions. There weren't many people who would invite a family of six to their home, but to people at Rabbit Hill, it wasn't an issue. Their grown daughters and their families would also be there, which meant stories and teasing for the whole afternoon. And pie ... lots of pie.

One thing we learned at Dave and Alma's farm was that Easter egg hunts did not require Easter eggs or chocolate of any kind. Cash was a better alternative for adults and soon-to-be adults. Money was hidden throughout the house in the most creative ways. I recall a $20 bill taped to the bottom of a kitchen drawer. Dave was thorough in hiding; the cash hunters were just as thorough in seeking.

Dave had some opinions about church, that included the music. As far as he was concerned, Colleen played the hymns too fast. Assuming the piano pedals were like the gas pedal of a car, he threatened to bring a block of wood to put under the pedal so that Colleen couldn't get up to third gear. Colleen tried to control the speed, but if a song had the opportunity for movement, she took advantage of it. I don't know if a block ever appeared, but the thought was there.

Alma and Dave had a wonderful rock garden on the farm. And by a rock garden, I mean rocks in the garden. They had collected big, beautiful rocks throughout their marriage. There were large chunks of petrified wood and other prizes. After Dave passed away, Alma put the farm up for sale. Before the new owner took possession, she invited people from the church who were rock lovers to come to the farm to pick up their favourites. We came away with a couple of beauties that we have heaved around with us in the years and moves since.

Auntie Alma moved into a new home in Leduc and continued to invite us on special occasions. Sometimes we tried to get everyone to our house, but somehow Alma won, and we ended up going to her place. We would contribute to the feast, counting on Auntie Alma's pie for dessert.

It was another Easter at Alma's when we learned more about Auntie Alma. We were carrying our contributions to the meal in the front door, down the hallway, and into the kitchen with Danica in the lead. She went into the kitchen first and came out looking like she was going to burst into laughter. I asked her what happened and all she could manage to say was, "Look at Auntie Alma's fridge."

I went in, calmly put the salad on the island, and turned to the fridge. Prominently placed on the fridge was the latest edition of the Edmonton Firefighters' Turn up the Heat calendar. I did not expect to see pictures of scantily clad firefighters in Alma's home. After all, she was over eighty! And a Baptist! And a Kuhn!

I took a breath and calmly asked, "Alma, tell me about your calendar." She shrugged her shoulders a little and said that her daughter, Leanne, had given it to her. "She said it was for charity."

Who could argue with that?

CHAPTER 14

A Rabbit Hill Welcome

THERE AREN'T MANY CHURCHES IN WESTERN CANADA old enough to have their own graveyard, but Rabbit Hill has one, as do the older Orthodox and Lutheran churches in the area.

Founding families of Rabbit Hill donated the land for both their church and cemetery; the Stelters provided the land for the church, and the Hillers did the same for the cemetery. The properties were not adjacent, which means that the cemetery is about a mile north of the church.

A tour through the cemetery gives every visitor a glimpse of who's who. Prominent Rabbit Hill families such as the Kuhns, Stelters, Hillers, and Rudolphs have their designated areas. A fringe benefit for former pastors is that they are given a spot if they so choose. Apparently, there are plots for Loren and me somewhere near the fence to the west when we need them. I'm in no hurry.

With each death in the church community, the men would gather to dig the grave. Lyle Stelter would bring over his backhoe to dig the initial hole and then the rest of the work would be done with shovels. Eventually, a ladder would be put into the grave and someone would have to go down to finish the walls so that the coffin could be gently lowered down.

Loren would accompany the digging team with a rough map of who was in the cemetery so they knew where to dig and hopefully not disturb any remains. Over the years, though, the ground shifted and things may have moved. Or as in the times of the flu epidemic or other outbreaks, graves were dug in a hurry and families may not have had the opportunity to mark the spot. Loren was there to keep safe any remains that the digging team may come across. This was another example of a pastoral responsibility that was not covered during seminary training.

After one grave digging episode, Loren came home chuckling and shaking his head. Dale Stelter had been in the grave finishing off the walls when he told Loren, "I'm done in here, Pastor. You can take the ladder out."

Loren looked down at him and asked, "Are you sure?"

"Yup, I'm done. You can take it out."

Again, Loren looked down at him and repeated: "Are you sure?"

It took a few minutes for Dale to register that he should probably exit the grave before the ladder was taken out. He made Loren promise that he would not mention the incident in a sermon. Even though it would have easily worked into a great sermon illustration, Loren kept his promise. His secret has stayed safe until now.

One day Loren received a call from a funeral director in Edmonton. He had a family whose mother had passed away and the family wanted her to be buried in our cemetery. Her daughter had often passed this pretty cemetery on her way from Edmonton to Devon and hoped she could have her mother buried there.

There weren't too many requests from people outside of the Rabbit Hill community, and since the cemetery was limited in space, the church leadership had to make a decision. Within a short period of time they came up with some guidelines for such requests, and the funeral director was informed that the family could have their mother buried in the Rabbit Hill Cemetery. Once again, the church trustees got together to decide on a suitable plot and start digging.

On the day of the funeral, Loren went to the cemetery to meet the family and offer his condolences. He was waiting when the funeral coach and the family arrived. A woman, presumably the daughter of the deceased, got out of the car and looked around in disbelief.

"This is the wrong cemetery!"

Her instructions to the funeral director hadn't been clear. She actually meant the cemetery southwest of Rabbit Hill that belonged to St. John's Lutheran. Despite the mix-up, we gave her mother a Rabbit Hill welcome.

CHAPTER 15

Uncle Ben and Auntie Lillie

WE HAVE WIND CHIMES BY OUR BACK DOOR THAT ARE a constant musical reminder of Uncle Ben's investment in the lives of the children at Rabbit Hill. The chimes were just one of the projects he had the kids build during Vacation Bible School over the years. The craft portion of a Vacation Bible School morning meant you built something useful. It wasn't just something flimsy that would take fifteen minutes to cut and glue together. No, it would take the whole week to build. It would last. It would be something you would be proud to take home.

Each year there was a new project. Usually Ben had a look at what he had on the farm and came up with an idea. Who else would have thought to cut up an old furnace to create a weather vane? I think it would have upset him to buy something new. There were always things on the farm you could use. Not only did Ben design these projects, but he would pre-cut and number the components and have everything ready for all age groups.

The older children would help the younger so that everyone had the same project. It also encouraged the kids to come back each day so they could have it done by Friday. Ben's building projects were a major draw for country and city kids alike.

Lillie also got to know the children at Rabbit Hill. She and her sister-in-law, Alma, taught Sunday school together for fifty years before they retired and let others take on the responsibility of the pre-schoolers. Both seemed surprised that it had been that long when the church recognized them for their long service. They just faithfully did what was asked of them, or, as Lillie would say, "I just did my level best."

Ben and Lillie were unassuming, modest people. Lillie baked her own bread. Jam for the bread was made from their garden's raspberries. Her cinnamon buns were second to none. Nothing was wasted. It makes me smile when I see her granddaughters posting pictures on Facebook of the pies they baked, the vegetables they canned, and the cookies they just pulled from the oven. Their grandmother would be so proud.

When Ben died the hymn "Am I a Soldier of the Cross?" kept playing on my internal soundtrack. Even though he was a quiet man, he just kept soldiering on through life. He worked hard, he stood up for what was right, and he raised his children to do the same.

A few years later when Auntie Lillie joined him in heaven, her children asked us to come back to Edmonton for the funeral. Loren preached and I was honoured to sing for Auntie Lillie one more time. Her song was always "His Eye Is on the Sparrow," and it suited her. When I got up to sing, I looked out over the packed church and it struck me that there were at least seven retired pastors in the crowd. They had started their ministry as student pastors at Rabbit Hill, and the friendship forged with Ben and Lillie in those early years had lasted for decades.

Just like everything else Ben built.

CHAPTER 16

An Extended Family

As I was driving the children to school one day we passed the construction site of a large church on Ellerslie Road. One of the kids said, "I wonder what it would be like to go to a big church like that?"

Danica said she didn't think it would be good.

"Why not?"

"In a big church like that we wouldn't know everyone, and they wouldn't know us."

Her reply stayed with me for a long time. Raising our children at Rabbit Hill was one of the best things we could have done for them. In a larger faith community, they would have easily been overlooked and they would not have the closer intergenerational friendships Rabbit Hill offered. A big church may have given them more friends their own age, but a small church provided a whole range of experiences and relationships they wouldn't have had elsewhere.

For the first seven years we lived in the parsonage next to the church and then, for a variety of reasons, we needed to move into the city. Even though we were a twenty-minute drive away (thirty minutes if I was driving), our friendships and activities continued as if we still lived next door.

It's not surprising that many denominational leaders grew up in small churches. In a small church everyone, children included, are expected to use their gifts and talents. At Rabbit Hill, any child past Grade 6 was expected to be a helper during Vacation Bible School. If you had any kind of musical ability, even if you could only play one song, your participation in the church was welcomed and applauded. You helped take the offering, assisted the little ones during junior church, shovelled snow in front of the church, or whatever needed to be done. The running of the church was everyone's responsibility. It mattered that you were there.

Our parents and siblings lived in other time zones, so the regular church members became our extended family. From the start older church members became "Auntie and Uncle" who were genuinely glad to see our children in church. They observed growth and gifts in our kids that we, as parents in our busy-ness, hadn't had time to notice.

I don't recall ever hearing or receiving criticism about our children's behaviour or choices. People in the church were just happy they were there. Whether they knew it or not, the Rabbit Hill congregation helped raise our children. They learned how to have conversations with people of various ages and backgrounds, and they were trusted to try new skills. They saw grown-ups who had enough life experience to know how healthy it was to laugh at themselves once in a while. Church was more than an hour together on Sunday mornings.

And because they were PK's (preacher's kids) they gained some helpful skills. If you didn't know an answer in Sunday school, you could invariably employ this one catch-all answer: "pray-read-your-Bible-go-to-church." Most Bible memory verses started with "And Jesus said ..." And the best skill to take you into adulthood: If you have no idea what is going on, you should just smile, nod, and back away.

CHAPTER 17

A Rabbit Hill Christmas

THE FIRST THING YOU NEED TO KNOW ABOUT CHRISTMAS at Rabbit Hill is that the Christmas Eve service is not on Christmas Eve. It never was and never will be. If you want to attend Rabbit Hill's Christmas Eve service, you need to be there on December 23. Even people in the neighbourhood who rarely come to church know this.

The pastor and his family did not know this. Not at first. When asked why December 23 was the favoured date, we were given two theories. The first was that in the early days the church shared a pastor with one of the Leduc or Edmonton churches. Since he couldn't be in two places at the same time for the Christmas celebration, the smaller, country church was assigned the earlier date so that he could make it to the larger "in town" church for the actual Christmas Eve date.

The other theory was that in years past, the young men at Rabbit Hill had married young women from other outlying country churches. These young wives became part of the Rabbit Hill church family for the whole Christian calendar, but on Christmas Eve they were adamant that they wanted to be with their home churches and families of origin. If the church wanted them to be there for a Christmas program, it would have to be on December 23.

Although this tradition felt odd at first, it freed us to attend a family Christmas service at another church on the 24th where we could sit together and enjoy hearing the story without having to be involved in the telling of it. It is a rare and wonderful thing for the pastor to be able to sit with his family without having to participate in the service. He didn't even have to close in prayer. We found churches where no one knew us, and we could attend incognito.

Preparation for the Rabbit Hill Christmas service would start at least a month earlier. There would be rehearsals for all the children on Saturday mornings where, most often, they were presented with a Rabbit Hill original script. Parts were assigned, costumes were chosen, and the music was practiced, accompanied by the usual chaos. I'd usually need a nap afterward, but somehow it all came together.

After the last rehearsal before the program when people knew more or less what they were going to do, everyone was invited to stay for a pizza lunch. While we ate, we listened for the tractor or horses that would take everyone out for the annual hayride. Kids were bundled in their snowsuits and off they went through the fields around the church. This was one of the biggest perks of learning your lines and enduring the rehearsals. Remarkably, everyone who left on the sled made it back.

On the 23rd, the whole neighbourhood showed up for the Christmas program. Extra chairs were set up at the back of the church and in the aisles; latecomers had to go up to the balcony. For many years the tree at the front of the church was donated by a local farmer. Those trees were massive. It took skill and strength to get the tree in place. The trees were so fresh that I expected to have a squirrel or other critter hop out during the program. If that had happened, I'm sure we could have made it look like we planned it that way.

One year I dared to write the whole program in rhyme. Everyone worked hard to learn their parts and when to say them. We all believed it could work. The children were all lined up in the church basement ready to make their entrance when a woman approached me with her little girl.

"She wants to be in the program; she wants to be an angel."

The child hadn't been to any of the rehearsals, but here she was, expecting to be part of the program. Although she was shy, we learned that she could say "Glory to God in the highest" along with the other angels. A costume was quickly found and she looked like she'd been at Rabbit Hill her whole life.

The other perk of being a kid at Rabbit Hill at Christmas was the treat bags they received at the end of the program. Whether they had memorized their lines or just attended that evening for the first time, all children were presented with one of those fabulous five-pound bags filled with chocolates, candy, and at least one mandarin orange. Rabbit Hill may be a small church, but they know how to do things in a big way. Christmas treat bags were one of those things.

After singing "Silent Night," people would file out, greeting one another and remarking that this was the best Christmas program yet. Downstairs the coffee was ready and the tables were loaded in preparation for the fellowship time that always followed the Christmas program. Grown-ups sat and talked while children darted about, hoping to get one more goodie before their parents realized how much they had already eaten. There's something solid about those evenings.

If you stood at the top of the stairs and listened, you would think it was a big family reunion. And you would be right.

CHAPTER 18

A Gift for Pastor Loren

EACH YEAR IT WAS THE SAME THING. A WEEK OR SO before Vacation Bible School, a wasps' nest would be spotted somewhere on the outside of the church. Somehow wasps knew that fifty to seventy-five children would be on the property, and they wanted to be part of the action.

Loren would walk around the church, and when he located the nest he would call our neighbour, Dale, who had a talent for disposing of such things. Loren would usually offer to help when there was something that needed fixing around the church, but when wasps, bees, or hornets were involved, he kept his distance. He hated them, and Dale was well aware of how Loren felt.

This time the nest was in the peak of the roof on the outside wall at the back of the building. We knew that Dale would wait until dusk when the wasps were home in their nest before he made his move. He brought over a ladder, wore long leather gloves, and carried an empty garbage bag.

I watched briefly from the window but then went back to the kitchen. Loren was downstairs with the kids when the front doorbell rang. It was Dale.

"Is Pastor here?" he asked with a big smile. I suspected that Dale had more than a smile to deliver.

I called Loren, who came up from the basement in a hurry thinking that something must have gone wrong.

"Hi Pastor—I've got a gift for you." Dale presented him with the black, plastic bag that now contained a wasps' nest and angry, recently woken wasps. He tried to hand it to Loren, but Loren kept his hands behind his back.

"Uh, no thanks, Dale. I appreciate the offer, though."

Dale laughed and took his bag of wasps back to his farm, where they met their end over a fire.

We appreciated all the gifts we received at Rabbit Hill. This one was one of the more memorable ones.

CHAPTER 19

Cornflakes in My Bed

There is something wonderful about turning off the gravel road and down Wesley and Delores' driveway. It always feels like coming home. Even if they aren't expecting us, there's a welcome at the door, and by the time we're in the kitchen, the coffee is on and we're already laughing.

It didn't take long for us to realize that serving at Rabbit Hill was going to be different than any other church we'd ever attended. Shortly after we moved into the parsonage, we invited the congregation for a housewarming party that included a house blessing. Together we asked God to bless the house and all who would come through the doors. Although that was a meaningful activity, what I remember most about that evening was going to bed later that night and finding cornflakes in our bed.

I knew immediately that Delores was involved. She didn't even try to deny it when I called her the next day to thank her for providing breakfast. I loved it that they treated us like friends that earned a bit of teasing … then and now. It was a sign that we belonged.

Wes and Delores may not have known how much we needed their laughter when we came to Rabbit Hill. They just carried on being themselves, which was what we needed. Delores started laughing one morning as we came out of church together. Her laughter was contagious, and I told her how much I needed a laugh like that. She replied with one of the great observations of the Rabbit Hill congregation.

"We laugh hard and we cry hard."

I still admire her balanced perspective on life.

When I asked our kids what they wanted to do during their first spring break in the country, they asked if they could go to a farm where they could jump around on hay bales. I'm not sure where they got this idea, but if it meant being outside after a long winter and it was free, it was a good plan. A quick phone call to Wes and Delores and we were off. Not only did they get to jump around on hay bales, but Auntie Delores took them to explore the creek behind their house. They saw evidence of beavers (not Delores' favourite animal) and witnessed a calf being born in the barn. Wes and Delores helped transform city kids to country kids. They were muddy and happy on the ride home.

Next to the house is Delores' vegetable garden. Every year I would hear, "I'm not planting that much this year; it's going to be smaller," and every year their garden looked massive. It wasn't possible for us to have a vegetable garden at the parsonage, and throughout the summer Delores generously shared her harvest. She also shared her kitchen so that we could make pickles together. In her kitchen pickles turned out beautifully. In my kitchen the pickles were not as successful—except when I used Delores' ice cream pail pickle recipe. No one could get that wrong.

Delores is the only woman I've met who was thrilled to get a chainsaw for Christmas. Not an ordinary gift for a woman, but then Delores is an extraordinary woman. The chainsaw meant she could deal with the fallen trees the beavers left behind on the creek banks. She was going to conquer the trail.

Even though her brother Dale had a bigger gun collection, he admitted that Delores was the better shot. There was a story circulating that Delores had taken her granddaughter out for a walk and shown her how to snare a gopher. Not wanting to kill the gopher on the spot, she and Katelyn walked the gopher home, where Delores promptly shot it. The beavers may also have been in her sights for their persistence in blocking up the creek, but nothing has ever been said on the matter. After all, the beaver is our national symbol and a protected animal.

There never seemed to be anything in the church that was too much of a challenge for Wes and Delores. It didn't matter how many children appeared at Vacation Bible School, Delores and her army of helpers made sure there was plenty of snacks for everyone. After all, the VBS snack was as important as the Bible lesson.

It took us some time to get used to the way decisions were made and carried out at Rabbit Hill. If something needed to get done, it got done—often without a board decision or a budget consideration. From what we could tell, an idea would come up on Sunday, on Monday there would be discussion over coffee, and by the end of the week a plan would already be in action.

For example: there was a suggestion that the parsonage needed a garage. Not only would it be helpful for the pastor to have shelter for his car, but it would be useful for the 100th anniversary celebrations. We needed a covered area from which to serve lunch after the Sunday morning service.

Almost before plans for the garage could be drawn up, Wes had a solution. Through one of his many connections in the county, he found large trusses that had been custom built, but the customer had never paid for them. Wes quickly arranged payment and delivery to the church yard. One weekend soon afterward, the men from the church built the garage that supported the trusses. When finished, the garage was large enough that we could drive our Honda Civic in circles inside of it. And of course, it happened to be just the right size for the food tables at the anniversary picnic.

Wesley and Delores have a remarkable marriage. It was no small matter for the congregation when Delores Stelter married Wesley Kuhn. While their marriage bridged two prominent families, it created a problem for the young couple. The Kuhns sat on one side of the church, and the Stelters on the other. Delores wondered if she and Wes would have to sit in the centre aisle just to keep both sides of the family happy. Somehow they managed to find a spot that worked, and when we arrived about forty years later, they could usually be found on the right side, about half way up, close to the window.

Loren describes Wes and Delores as having unflappable faith. Whatever happened in the church or in their family, they seemed to take it in stride and keep going. They continue to find practical ways to serve, encourage others, and keep the church doors open.

And if Delores is there, she will have pie.

Apple pie.

CHAPTER 20

Saying Goodbye

LOREN HAD KNOWN FOR SOME TIME THAT HE HAD FULfilled his mandate at Rabbit Hill. It was time for someone else to lead the congregation. Although it would be difficult for us to leave these dear people, God had been leading him to keep his heart open to new possibilities. We did not share this with the congregation until the time was right.

I needed a little more direct intervention. At the end of each Sunday morning service, the congregation would sing a hymn and, after the first verse, Loren would pronounce the benediction and leave the platform while the congregation sang the rest of the hymn. I would be seated on the aisle (on the piano side) and Loren would pause on his way to the back of the sanctuary so that I could join him in greeting everyone on their way out of the sanctuary. We jokingly referred to this as "the kiss line." Actually, it was more like "the hug line."

It was an autumn morning in 2003 when we had finished greeting and hugging people that I returned to get my purse and Bible from where I had been sitting. I reached to get my things, and even though there was no one else in the sanctuary, I felt a hand on my shoulder, gently nudging me to sit down. Although I didn't hear the words audibly, I could clearly hear them in my heart.

"You're going to have to get ready to say goodbye."

I sighed. I had just received compassionate fair warning of what was to come. After twelve years with these people, this was going to be difficult. I kept the message between us and trusted that I would be ready for whatever came next.

Early in 2004, Loren was in Vancouver for two weeks working on his Doctorate at Carey Theological College. He was staying with my parents when he received a call from Erwin Kujat, our denomination's regional minister, in British Columbia. Erwin asked Loren if he might be interested in serving a multi-cultural church in Vancouver. Loren went to visit Pilgrim Baptist on a Sunday morning and was intrigued by the congregation. Further conversations with the church leadership followed, and later in the spring Loren resigned as Rabbit Hill's senior pastor.

One of the things I knew we would miss from Rabbit Hill was their spontaneous singing. If they knew a song that was being played by the organ and piano in the prelude or offertory, they sang along. Even if they didn't know the song, they would peer over Colleen and Bea's shoulders to get the number out of the hymnal so they had the words. Knowing this was precious to us, they presented Loren and me with one of their hymnals as a goodbye card. For a few weeks prior to our last service, the hymnal was circulated so that people could sign their names next to their favourite hymn. It was the best goodbye card we've ever received.

The church would miss us, but Loren had been mentoring the church's youth pastor, Lee Dyck, to move into the role of senior pastor. The congregation saw this as God's leading and unanimously asked Lee to take over the reins. The transition from one pastor to another was amazingly smooth.

Pilgrim called Loren to begin his ministry with them on July 1, 2004. We were excited about this, but it meant a year of transition for our family. Our children were all close to important milestones in their education. After talking and praying about it, we decided that I would stay in Edmonton with the children so that Alita could finish off her degree at Taylor College, Danica could complete her second year of Pre-Vet studies at the University of Alberta, Daniel could graduate from Strathcona High, and Jonathan could get another year at L.Y. Cairns School, which offered the specialized courses he needed. We arranged that Loren would fly back to Edmonton every five weeks, and we talked by phone every day.

The kids and I were given another year with our Rabbit Hill family.

The Sunday after Loren left for Vancouver, Rabbit Hill held its annual church picnic. The weather looked ominous but we went ahead with plans, as Albertans are known to do. Alita and

Danica left the picnic early while Daniel, Jonathan, and I stayed at the church a little longer. The distant thunder got louder and we all ran for cover when the rains came. The girls phoned in a panic; the storm had hit the city with vengeance. There was water in our basement and it was rising quickly. We jumped in our car and raced to Edmonton, avoiding the low-lying roads that had suddenly flooded. I had to park about a block away from our house because our cul-de-sac was completely submerged. The water was creeping up our driveway where the girls were waiting for us.

"Look, Mom, we have waterfront property."

Things were bad and they were getting worse. Water was coming into the basement, flooding Danica's bedroom, my study area, and the laundry room. We rescued her drum set and a few other treasures before the water seeped up the stairs. We were within inches of having our family room and Alita's room under water as well.

Danica and Daniel waded out to the car and drove to the golf course where they had been working that summer to borrow a pump. A second pump appeared with our Rabbit Hill friends, Dale and Gladys and Wes and Delores. They literally bailed us out that day. Even while pumping water out of the house there was laughter and assuring hugs. The situation was difficult but we were going to be okay. Loren was on the phone from Vancouver feeling helpless and still had to concentrate on preaching a sermon that evening. It gave him immense peace of mind to know that our Rabbit Hill family had come to our rescue.

Our neighbours, who were also flooded, were amazed at the quick support we'd received from our friends. They weren't just ordinary friends—they were our Rabbit Hill family. They are people who come to your rescue before you can ask. And they have stayed in our hearts ever since.

CHAPTER 21

Potluck Recipes

Apple Cinnamon French Toast

This is what I would contribute to the Missions Potluck Breakfast. Thank you to whoever gave me the recipe. It's still a Stark family favourite and is requested when everyone comes home at Christmas.

Day before:

> 5 tbsp. butter
> 2 large baking apples—cored and sliced
> 1 cup brown sugar
> 2 tbsp. corn syrup
> 1 tsp. cinnamon
> 8 one-inch slices French bread (or day old whatever-kind of bread)
> 3 large eggs *
> 1 cup milk *
> 1 tsp. vanilla*

- Melt butter over medium heat. Add apple slices and cook until tender.

- Add brown sugar, corn syrup, and cinnamon; cook until sugar dissolves.

- Pour mixture into a greased 13 x 9 baking dish.

- Arrange bread slices on top.

- Beat together eggs, milk, and vanilla until well mixed; pour over bread.

- Cover with plastic wrap and refrigerate overnight.

Next day:

- Remove plastic wrap and bake at 375 F for 30–35 minutes. Cool in pan.
- Dust with icing sugar.

SHORT CUT

When you forget or are too tired the night before:

- Grease a 13 x 9 dish
- Dump in 2 cans apple pie filling (any other kind of pie filling works too).
- Add bread slices.
- Continue with mixing eggs, milk, and vanilla.
- Bake as above.

Auntie Lillie Kuhn's Most Excellent Ginger Snaps

---

1 cup sugar

¾ cup butter or margarine

2 scant cups flour

¼ cup chopped crystalized ginger

1 egg

2 tbsp. light molasses

½ tsp. ground ginger

1 ½ tsp. cinnamon

1 tsp. baking soda

- In a large bowl with mixer at high speed beat sugar and butter or margarine until light and fluffy.

- Add egg and beat a bit more.

- Reduce speed to low; beat in molasses.

- Put in flour and remaining ingredients until well mixed, scraping bowl with spatula.

- Shape dough into ball, cover, and put in fridge until dough is firm enough to handle.

- Preheat oven to 375° F.

- Scoop out 1 level tbsp. and shape into balls.

- Place 3 inches apart on ungreased cookie sheet.

- With the bottom of glass dipped in sugar, flatten to about 2-inch rounds.

- Bake cookies about 10–12 minutes until golden brown.

- Put on rack to cool.

- Makes about 3 dozen cookies.

Auntie Lillie's Cinnamon Buns

Auntie Lillie baked these and homemade bread until the very end. Here's her recipe as shared by her daughter, Lyla. I have not attempted to make these yet because I don't have a mixing bowl big enough! Lyla added these instructions:

Raisins were always optional as some did not like them. She put ¼ cup brown sugar and ¼ cup cream and a bit of vanilla in the bottom of the pan. She dipped the top of the dough into the mixture before she put them in to rise.

---

2 quarts milk, scalded

Add ¾ cup butter and 1 cup sugar; cool to warm.

2 tsp. sugar

1 cup lukewarm water

2 tbsp. (rounded) yeast

Combine and let stand 10 minutes.

12 room temperature eggs, beaten

Mix all ingredients above together.

20 cups all purpose flour

4 tsp. salt

4 cups raisins (raisins should be considered optional since Auntie Lillie didn't like them and didn't often add them)

- Add liquid mixture to flour. Knead till smooth and slightly sticky. When just about finished add raisins and work some more. Grease sides and top of large mixing bowl with butter. Let dough rise until doubled in bulk.

> 2 cups poppy seeds that have been washed with boiling water and drained well.
>
> 1 cup brown sugar
>
> ¼ cup cream
>
> 1 tsp. cinnamon
>
> Bring to a boil and cool.

· Knead dough down and form into loaf sized pieces. Stretch into rectangular shape. Smear with a little melted butter. Spread with 2 tbsp. poppy seed mixture, brown sugar, and cinnamon. Pull up or braid and place in pans. Let rise until doubled in size.

· Bake at 350° F for 10 minutes then to 325° F (dough burns easily) for 30 additional minutes. When done and still hot, brush with a mixture of

> 1 cup cream
>
> ½ cup brown sugar
>
> vanilla

Delores' Apple Pie

Preparing pie was a project that involved the whole family. The apples came from Minnie, Bea, and Hazel's tree in the city. Delores would make the crust, Bea would roll it out, and Hazel and Minnie would peel and slice the apples. Delores and her daughter, Karen, and Karen's kids would assemble the pies and put them into the freezer. Their one-day pie-making record was 125.

Big batch never fail pie crust:

Makes approximately 12 two-crust pies.

---

12 cups flour
4 cups lard (Tenderflake is best)
½ cup butter or margarine
2 cups water (very cold)
4 tsp. salt
4 tsp. vinegar

- Mix the flour, salt, lard, and butter together until crumbly; add vinegar to water and then add to the flour mixture in small amounts until it feels "elastic" and like pie crust. Roll out thin and always roll from the middle out, each direction on a lightly floured surface. You may freeze it in pie plates or in a lump for later use.

Filling

- Have someone peel and slice apples for you; sprinkle 2 tsp. of flour on the crust then put the apples on. Sprinkle sugar (¼–½ cup) on apples in pie shell, shake cinnamon on to taste. Dot butter on top then put top crust on.

- Put whatever kind of fruit you want in with the apples to change it up a bit.

- Bake at 350° F until done. Pies may also be frozen raw and baked from frozen.

Alma Kuhn's Heavenly Lemon Pie

Pastry for 2 crusts—use one crust and freeze the other.

½ lb. shortening
1 tsp. baking powder
1 tsp. salt
Mix until crumbly; slowly add:
½ cup boiling water
stir in 3 cups flour

· Knead until smooth. Roll out and put in 9 inch pie plate and bake until golden brown.

Filling:

½ cup sugar
⅓ cup cornstarch
⅓ tsp. salt
1 ½ cups water
Cook until thickened. Then add:
2 tbsp. grated lemon zest
¼ cup lemon juice
3 tbsp. butter
Beat 4 egg yolks.

· Add some of the hot mixture to the egg yolks then add to the filling and cook and beat until thickened.

- Pour into baked crust.

Meringue:

- Beat 4 egg whites with ¼ tsp. Cream of Tartar until peaks form

- Slowly add ⅔ cup sugar

- Add dash of salt

- Put on top of filling

- Bake until golden brown.

Homemade Oreos

I am so grateful to Carolyn Roth for sharing this recipe with me years ago. A double batch would be just enough for the annual Rabbit Hill young moms' cookie exchange. It's still a family favourite. It doesn't feel like we're ready for Christmas unless we've had an Oreo-baking day.

---

2 pkg. devil's food cake mix
4 eggs
⅔ cup oil

- Mix, roll into balls (size of egg yolk). Don't flatten.
- Bake at 350° F for 8–10 minutes or until they crack.
- Cool.

Filling:

One 8 oz. pkg. Philly Cream Cheese
¼ cup margarine or butter
1 tsp. vanilla
3 ½ cups icing sugar (may need more)

- Beat together, adding the icing sugar as needed. Spread a generous amount between 2 cookies.

Oma's Streusel Kuchen

My mother (Oma) would sometimes refer to this as "Beerdigung's Kuchen," or funeral cake, because you usually had all the ingredients on hand and you could make it quickly and bring to someone in crisis. A German (or at least Oma) would never show up at a funeral or crisis without a cake. A German without a kuchen IS a crisis!

- Preheat oven to 350° F

Mix together:

> ⅓ cup veg. oil
> 3 eggs
> 1 cup sugar
> 1 ½ cups milk

Mix separately:

> 3 cups flour
> 4 tsp. baking powder

- Add flour mixture to oil mixture. Spread in a greased 9 x 13 pan.

- Optional—spread some blueberries or other fresh/frozen fruit on top.

Struesel:

Mix together until crumbly:

> 1 cup sugar
>
> 1 cup butter or margarine (cold)
>
> 1 ½ cups flour

- Sprinkle on top of base/fruit.
- Bake at 350° F for 40 minutes or until toothpick comes out clean.

Potluck Baked Beans

This was given to us by Loren's mom, Irma Stark. It was a favourite for potlucks and family reunions. Don't leave out the pineapple—it's the secret ingredient that prevents the toots afterwards. For years Mom Stark would time her visits to us with the annual church picnic. This would be her contribution.

---

3 cans of beans in tomato sauce
1 small can pineapple tidbits or crushed, drained
1 sausage ring (Ukrainian sausage) cut up
1 onion chopped
¼ cup brown sugar
4–5 slices chopped bacon (optional)

- Spray Pam in slow cooker; add remaining ingredients. Cook on low for 4–5 hrs.
- Serve with crusty bread or buns.

Pulled Pork

---

1 pork roast, any cut
1 large onion, sliced
2 tbsp. Worcestershire sauce
2 cups water
Later: 1 bottle (16-oz.) barbecue sauce

- Place pork roast, sliced onion, water, and Worcestershire sauce in slow-cooker. Turn on low and cook for 10 to 12 hours, until roast is fork tender (shreds easily when inserting a fork).

- Remove pork from slow-cooker; discard water. Fork shred pork, discarding any fat and bones. Return to slow-cooker. Add 1 full bottle of your favourite barbecue sauce.

- Cook on low for 1–2 hours.

- Serve on rolls with salad of your choice as a side dish.

Delores' Ice Cream Pail Pickles

- Soak washed cucumbers in cold brine water with handful of pickling salt for 1 hour.

- Drain.

- Slice the cucumbers to fill the ice cream pail almost full.

Brine:

---

4 cups sugar

2 tbsp. pickling salt

4 cups vinegar

1 1/3 tsp. turmeric

1 1/3 tsp. mustard seed

- Mix all together. DO NOT HEAT THE BRINE

- Pour cold brine over the cucumbers, stir, and refrigerate. Stir occasionally for 5 days. Keep in fridge for 8 months. When pail is half empty, fill with new sliced cucumbers at bottom. Don't add more vinegar. This can be repeated 3–4 times before new brine is made.

CPSIA information can be obtained
at www.ICGtesting.com
Printed in the USA
BVHW030534081220
595126BV00011B/94